Contents

Our clothes

The clothes people wear tell us a lot about who they are and where they live.

People who live in hot parts of the world wear clothes that keep them cool, like T-shirts and shorts made from cotton.

Hats offer shade from a hot, burning sun.

clothes
around the world

Godfrey Hall

HODDER
Wayland

an imprint of Hodder Children's Books

Titles in this series:
Clothes Around the World
Festivals Around the World
Food Around the World
Houses Around the World
Musical Instruments Around the World
Shops and Markets Around the World
Toys and Games Around the World
Transport Around the World

Cover pictures: (Clockwise from top) Children in Hawaii wearing flowers. A Canadian boy wearing clothes made of animal skin and fur. Women in India wearing sandals to keep their feet cool. A girl from Peru wearing an *aguayo*, a heavy woollen shawl, to keep her warm.

Contents page: Children in school uniform in Malaysia.

Series editor: Deb Elliott
Book design: Malcolm Walker
Cover design: Simon Balley

First published in Great Britain in 1995
by Wayland (Publishers) Ltd

Reprinted in 2000 by Hodder Wayland,
an imprint of Hodder Children's Books

© Hodder Wayland 1995

Hodder Children's Books, a division of Hodder Headline Ltd
338 Euston Road, London NW1 3BH

British Library Cataloguing in Publication Data
Hall, Godfrey
    Clothes. – (Around the World Series)
    I. Title II. Series
    391

ISBN 0 7502 2558 0

Typeset by Kudos Design Services
Printed and bound in Italy by G. Canale & C.S.p.A.

With thanks to Mike Theobald, Ennaimi Hazzim Abbas, King Fahad Academy, Dusseldorf Tourist Office, Joan and Harold Vidler.

Acknowledgements
The publishers would like to thank the following for allowing their pictures to be reproduced in this book: APM 9; Damart 12; Eye Ubiquitous 4 (bottom, Tim Page), 6 (Philip Quirk),11 (Tim Page), 17 (Frank Leather), 22 (bottom, Greg Iland), 28 (bottom, Sean Aidan); Sally and Richard Greenhill 13; Robert Harding Picture Library 29 (bottom); Zul Mukhida 14 (top); Rex Features *contents page* (Patsy Fagan), top right *cover* and 5 (top, Eric Peltier) (bottom, A. Bradshaw), 7 (top, Maria Muinos), 10 (top, Philippe Millereau), 14 (bottom), 15 (top, Philip Goodliff), 20 (top), 22 (top), 23 (Nadai), 24 (both, Michael Friedel), 26, 29 (top, Brendan Beirn); Peter Sanders 10 (bottom); Tony Stone Worldwide bottom right cover, bottom left *cover* (Michael Scott), top left *cover* (Art Brewer), 4 (top, Tony Craddock), 8, 14, 18 (Michael Scott), 19, 20 (Doug Armand), 21 (Richard Passmore), 27 (top, Art Brewer), 28 (top); Alison Thomson 16 (bottom); Julia Waterlow 16 (top), 25, 27 (bottom).

In cold parts of Canada, people wear clothes made from animal skins and fur.

Wearing lots of layers of clothes is another good way to keep warm in cold weather.

Hats

In hot countries, like Australia, people often wear hats with wide brims to protect them from the strong sunshine.

In the cold mountains of Peru, women wear thick, woollen hats which keep their heads warm.

Many boys who follow the Jewish religion wear a skullcap, called a *yarmulke*, from the age of three.

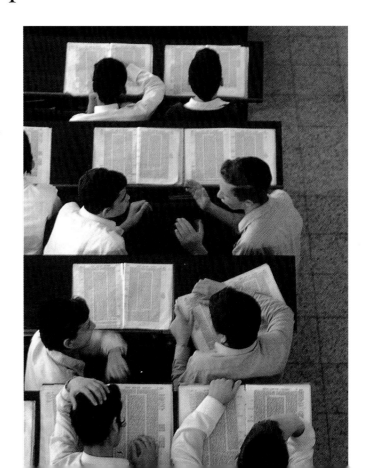

Shoes

In hot countries, such as India, women may wear sandals made from leather or rubber. Sandals let lots of cool, fresh air get to the feet.

Trainers are very popular with young people all over the world. These fashionable sports shoes are comfortable and look good.

Outdoor clothes

Children in Norway enjoy skiing in the snow. They wear padded anoraks and thick trousers, and gloves to keep their hands warm.

In hot countries, such as Saudi Arabia, people often wear white cotton clothes. These reflect the heat and keep them cool.

10

In Vietnam many people wear flowing cotton shirts and loose trousers. These clothes let air move around their bodies and are comfortable in hot weather.

Underwear

In very cold parts of the world people often wear thermal underwear. This is made of a special material which traps heat around the body and keeps it warm.

In Britain, children may have gym lessons wearing cotton vests and pants. This keeps them cool when doing lots of exercise.

Baby clothes

In many parts of the world, babies are dressed in all-in-one outfits with socks attached to them. These make the babies feel warm, snug and safe.

People sometimes wear special 'baby-carriers' attached to their backs or fronts. These help the baby to feel safe and snug against the mother or father's body.

In Guatemala, a mother may carry her baby in a brightly coloured shawl when she goes to the market.

Special occasions

People often dress up for festivals and religious occasions.

These Chinese men have dressed up in special costumes and have decorated their boat as part of the Dragon Boat festival.

In Indonesia, girls dress in black to celebrate weddings.

In Japan, the traditional kimono is worn by men and women at special events. It is a type of loose dress tied with a cord.

Traditional clothes

The weather can be very cold in Peru. Women and girls wear heavy woollen shawls called *aguayos*.

These Greek guards are wearing *fustanellas*, or kilts, which are their national costume.

Dressing up

During carnival time, children in Germany and The Netherlands dress up as clowns or wear funny hats.

Carnivals in the Caribbean and South America are very colourful and spectacular.

On the first Monday in May, English dancers known as Morris dancers wear white shirts and trousers decorated with ribbons and bells to celebrate the coming of summer.

Hot weather clothes

In hot weather, children love playing on the beach. They may wear just a swimsuit or shorts and a sunhat.

The sun in Australia can be very strong. People wear coloured sunscreen to protect their skin.

In Saudi Arabia women wear a flowing black cape called an *abaya*.

Cold weather clothes

When the weather is cold, we wear clothes that keep us snug and warm.

Lapland is an area of northern Europe. People who live there wear clothes made from reindeer skin to protect them from the ice-cold weather.

This boy lives in Quebec in Canada. His thick, furry hat keeps his ears and head warm and cosy.

These Chinese children live in the snowy Tibetan Plateau. They are wearing layers of clothes to keep themselves warm. They include vests, T-shirts, jumpers and coats.

Bits and bobs

People all over the world enjoy wearing jewellery. Indian women may wear nose rings and earrings.

In Hawaii children decorate their hair and make necklaces using flowers.

This girl comes from the Guizhou Province in China. She is wearing silver necklaces and decorations in her hair.

Sportswear

Some baseball players wear a special helmet and gloves to protect themselves from the hard ball.

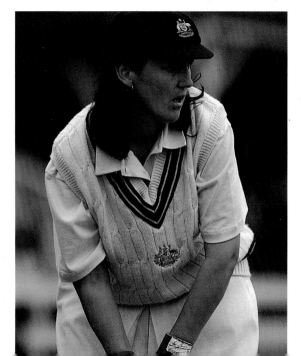

Cricketers usually wear white clothes, because they show up well against the green grass.

Surfers wear special suits which keep their bodies warm when they spend a long time in the water.

Ice hockey is a fast game. The players wear helmets and padded clothing to protect themselves from the ice and from contact with other players.

Glossary

anorak   A warm waterproof coat.

carnival   A festival when people enjoy themselves.

embroidered   Decorated with fancy stitches.

fustanellas   A white, knee-length skirt worn by men in Greece.

kilt   A knee-length, pleated skirt.

Morris dancers   English dancers who usually perform with sticks and bells.

sunscreen   Cream that protects the skin from burning.

thermal   Warm.

wet suits   Tight rubber suits that keep swimmers and surfers warm in the cold water.

Books to read

Country Fact Files: Japan by John Baines (Macdonald Young, 1994)
Focus on Greece by Dicks (Hamish Hamilton, 1988)
Philip's Children's Atlas by David and Jill Wright (Heinemann, 1996)
The Usborne Book of World Geography (Usborne, 1993)

More information

Would you like to know about the people and places you have seen in the photographs in this book? If so, read on.

pages 4–5
Girl dressed in T-shirt and shorts, pictured with Pluto at Disney World in Florida. Florida is on the south-east coast of the USA and the weather is warm all year round.
Children at a market in Dien Bien Phu, Taiwan. Taiwan is an island off the south-east coast of China.
Canadian Indian boy dressed in clothes made from animal skins to keep warm.
Little Tibetan boy dressed in warm clothes. Tibet is a high mountainous region of south-west China.

pages 6–7
Man wearing a sunhat at a cricket match in Sydney, Australia.
Women embroidering patterns on to material in the village of Ile Los Urus in Peru. Peru is on the west coast of South America.
Yarmulkes are worn during prayer by very religious Jewish boys and men.

pages 8–9
These women are from Rajasthan in northern India. They are wearing saris, the traditional dress of women from India and Pakistan. A sari is a long piece of coloured material which is wrapped around the body.
Trainers are worn not only for sport, but for fashion and comfort too.

pages 10–11
Norway is a country in northern Europe. Winters are very cold in Norway; the country is covered with snow and ice for many months. People have to dress up warmly.
Children in the Gassim region of Saudi Arabia. People in hot countries often wear white clothes because the colour reflects heat. This means that the heat is thrown back.
Vietnam is a country in South-East Asia.

pages 12–13
Thermal material traps heat.
Gym class at a school in north London, England.

pages 14–15
Babygros have popper buttons along each leg and across the bottom to make it easy to change the baby's nappy.
Parents have always carried their babies in slings or backpacks. Babies find it very comfortable and it leaves the carrier's hands free to carry shopping or to do some gardening, for example.
This Guatemalan mother is able to shop at the market while carrying her baby in a shawl.

pages 16–17
At the Dragon Boat festival, boats decorated with dragons' heads are raced.
Indonesia is a group of over 3000 small islands in South-East Asia.
These women are wearing the traditional Japanese kimono as part of the Hollyhock festival.

pages 18–19
The traditional costume of Peru.
Soldiers guarding the Tomb of the Unknown Soldier in Athens, Greece.

pages 20–21
Taking part in the Retro carnival in Cologne, Germany.
This magnificent costume was worn during carnival time in Port of Spain, Trinidad.
Morris dancers in Yorkshire, England. The dancers dress up to celebrate spring.

pages 22–23
Keeping cool at the seaside in shorts.
It is very important to wear sunscreen when you go out in strong sunshine. Sunscreen comes in different strengths, to suit all types of skin.
These Saudi Arabian women follow the Muslim religion. They have covered themselves up as part of their religious beliefs.

pages 24–25
Quebec is in the east of Canada. The winter is bitterly cold, so it is important to wear clothes made from warm materials.
Lapland is an area of northern Europe. People who live there wear clothes made from reindeer skin to protect them from the ice-cold weather.
The weather in China is extreme; it is freezing cold in the north and sub-tropical in the south of the country.

pages 26–27
Running along a beautiful Hawaiian beach. Hawaii is part of the USA; it is an island off the west coast, in the Pacific Ocean.
Chinese girl wearing jewellery and clothes which are traditional to the region she comes from.

pages 28–29
Behind the player with the bat sits the catcher, and behind the catcher crouches the umpire, in this game of baseball.
Julie Calvert batting for the Australian women's cricket team.
Surfers testing the waves on Bondi Beach in Sydney, Australia.
Ice hockey is played by two teams of six players.

Index